buddha's
dogs

Funding for the 2002 Intro Prize in Poetry
was provided in part by a generous donation
in memory of John J. Wilson.

To May, with love and joy Arf! Arf! Susan

buddha's dogs

Susan Browne

Susan Browne 6/04

Four Way Books
New York City

Distributed by
University Press of New England
Hanover and London

Editorial Office
Four Way Books
POB 535, Village Station
New York, NY 10014
www.fourwaybooks.com

Library of Congress Catalogue Card Number: 2002116858

ISBN 1-884800-56-4

Cover art: Brian Rumbolo

This book is manufactured in the United States of America and printed
on acid-free paper.

Four Way Books is a division of Friends of Writers, Inc., a Vermont-based
not-for-profit organization. We are grateful for the assistance we receive
from individual donors and private foundations.

Distributed by University Press of New England
One Court Street, Lebanon, NH 03766

ACKNOWLEDGMENTS

Grateful acknowledgment is made to the editors of the following publications in which these poems, or versions of them, first appeared:

"At Mountain View Cemetery": *Southern Poetry Reveiw,* Spring/Summer, 2003

"After Breaking-Up with My Twenty-Seventh Boyfriend": *Mississippi Review,* Spring, 2003

"Swearing, Smoking, Drinking": *Gargoyle,* Winter, 2003

"Ode to High School, 1966–1970": *River City,* Winter, 2002

"Love Match": *Clackamas Literary Review,* Fall, 2001

"Buddha's Dogs": *Sad Little Breathings & Other Acts of Ventriloquism,* PublishingOnline, Fall, 2001

"Smoke": *National Poetry Competition Winners 1999,* Chester H. Jones Foundation

"Father's Day": *The Sun,* Chapel Hill, North Carolina, February, 1999

"To My Night Pals": *1999 Oakland Renaissance,* Virgo Rising Press, Oakland, California

"Dear John"and "Star Food Sonata": *Alaska Quarterly Review,* Vol. 17, No. 1 & 2, 1998

"When My Mother Meets God," published as "Poem in My Mother's Voice": *The Poet's Companion, A Guide To the Pleasures of Writing Poetry,* W.W. Norton, 1997

"The Chair": *Diverse Voices of Women,* Mayfield Publishing Company, Mountain View, California, 1994

"Russian River" is after Billy Collins' poem, "Canada"

Thanks to: Jessica Barksdale Inclán, Martha Rhodes, Maureen and Jim Baumgartner, Clark McKowen, and Anita Feder-Chernila.

And especially: Kim Addonizio for her *duende,* inspiration, and critical comments.

To Kenneth Jensen: *Jeg elsker dig og ja jeg vil sove med dig i nat.*

for my sisters, Cheryl and Kerry

CONTENTS

There are love-dogs
no one knows the names of.

Give your life
to be one of them.

– Rumi

I

GENESIS

"Bless me, Father, for I have sinned:
I bit my sister on the arm,

took the Lord's name in vain, and
where do babies come from?"

Behind the dented screen,
Father Sebastian sighed.

Then with God's weighty authority
he said, "They come from a kiss. A germ

passes from the man to the woman,
travels down the esophagus

into the stomach where a baby is made."
After that, when Dad tried to kiss me,

I twisted my face like a gargoyle,
his lips skidding off my nose.

"She's going through a phase," Mom said,
but it lasted until sixth grade science.

Mr. Conklin had a passion for truth
and lectured zealously

about the penis entering the vagina,
drawing a hailstorm of sperm on the board,

with one like a lightning bolt
that split the ovum and made a zygote,

which turned into a fetus and then a baby.
An equal sign followed each drawing

to show how it added up. I raised my hand
and asked to go to the bathroom

where I sat on the toilet in the clammy dark,
nauseated and amazed at the revelation:

Father Sebastian and Mr. Conklin
had come from zygotes, from shocked eggs

like the ones nesting in my body,
waiting for the deluge.

I AM CYRANO

I marvel that this matter, shuffled pell-mell at the whim of Chance,
could have made a man.

— *Cyrano de Bergerac*

Beyond my nose, out the window:
the blaze of bougainvillea
that could be me, magenta nebula
with gold stamen star in the middle.
This skin and bone,
on its way to being skin and bone,
might have stopped and changed its mind
a trillion times, and maybe it did:
I could have been a cabbage,
an igneous rock, a walrus.
And I must have been here before,
wanting so much to be here again
I practically killed my mother
getting out of her.
I marvel like you, Cyrano,
at this matter
that is, sooner or later,
shuffled pell-mell
at the whim of Chance
into everything.

RUSSIAN RIVER

I am writing this on Richie Cooper's underwear
that my sister and Richie's sister froze
in the basement freezer
of the vacation cabin our families shared.

I am writing this with a banana slug,
one of the boneless flock oozing along
the mildewed walls of the basement shower
where we washed off the river sand.

There is no other way to express
the splendor of those summers,
the days' endless splash and swim,
holding our breath as long as we could

in the green underworld
where death was only
what a very old great uncle did
in a far away country like New Jersey.

O Russian River,
you are redwood and blue pine,
The Hundred Stairs we counted
up the hill of poison oak.

You are hotdogs and Frosty Cones,
licorice scent of sunlight on skin.
You are the cornball talent show
at Odd Fellows Hall,

slow dancing at Rio Nido, sweaty palms,
parents leaning through the open windows,
my Catholic mother yelling,
"Play a fast one!"

You are my bad-boy father
teaching me tennis in Guerneville:
"Bend, reach, hit the sweet spot."
You are Richie's sister ironing her hair,

the marijuana we sprinkled on the lasagna.
You are song,
the stacks of 45's: *Louie, Louie;*
Woolly Bully; Wild Thing;

my sister lip-syncing
Hold Me, Thrill Me, Kiss Me,
eyes closed and dreaming of The One
she'll marry soon, taking her away from me.

You are the screened-in porch,
its row of twin beds where we kids slept,
Richie having his revenge,
putting salamanders in our sleeping bags.

You are before sex,
before our lives claimed us.
You are *I Wanna Hold Your Hand,*
and I will never forget you,

O Russian River,
though I am writing this now on the water,
my words flowing swiftly
down your dark current to the sea.

THE BOY WHO HATED EMILY DICKINSON

In the middle of a discussion about imagery, the student says
he doesn't think Emily Dickinson is a very good poet.

He is eighteen years old and has read three poems
during his academic career: the famous one by Frost

about the road, (it's ok, he likes the rhyme scheme);
the one by Tennyson, (his favorite poet of all time),

about a flower hanging out of a wall;
and the one by Emily Dickinson that he can't remember

but totally and completely hated.
"If you need a Master's Degree and a Ph.D. to understand

her poems, how clear can they be?" He juts his jaw,
smooth as a dewy peach, at me.

"What's so great about her anyway?"
I decide that I have made a mistake,

treating my students like human beings,
allowing them to talk, and acting human myself

instead of like a bloodless egghead with my degrees
crammed up my ass. I vow, from now on,

to wear a three-piece suit, support hose, my hair in a tight bun,
carry a whip, and lecture nonstop, filling the board

with Roman numerals and polysyllabic information
to be regurgitated weekly on the blue-book exam.

What I do, though, is try to answer the student's question
by reciting one of Emily Dickinson's poems, (a short one),

and saying briefly yet passionately—and, hopefully,
not pretentiously—why I love it,

but his eyelids droop before I finish the first line.
I watch him sleep.

His life right now must be so heavy—
not a thing with feathers, and doesn't sing—at all.

TO THE POSTMODERN POET

We would like your poem to have a dazzling surface
and very little narrative. It would be best

if you don't mention yourself or anyone you know,
especially your family. If there must be a frame

on which to drape this scintillating missive
from beyond the comprehensible galaxy,

make it as invisible as the bones of God,
a diaphanous riddle, perhaps, about the shadow

of a shadow of a bug. We would appreciate it
if the point of view is from language to language alone,

and would highly esteem each erudite word drifting
indeterminately around and around the cerebral cortex,

gathering into a dense but brilliant fog as impenetrable
as a steel vault. We would prefer this poem unreadable

so it is not soiled by the messy understanding
of the human world.

Along with the blinding surface,
let its depth plummet into the silence

of one billion billion years after the obliteration of all
known and unknown universes,

a receding radio signal
going nowhere.

ON LEARNING RATS NEST IN TREES

At the top of the sweet cherry
or seraphic plum,
even in ragged palms
along the cracked median

on the causeway
that leads to the dump—
wait a minute—
aren't rats subterranean?

Don't they prefer the graveyard,
scurrying around,
wallowing in decay?
What do I know of life?

Perhaps rats like to sunbathe,
need those ultraviolet rays
to help stave off depression,
lifting their feral faces

to feel creation's favor,
whiskers twitching with pleasure.
As a child, I loved the laddering trees,
climbing as high as I could

to get a better view.
Then I'd rest,
vitamin D pouring
through the branches,

each leaf a small blaze
of photosynthesis,
warming my skin.
I would live forever.

What is heaven?
Is it like nesting at the top
of the tallest, greenest
palm tree by the sea?

All-inclusive,
a plague of luminous creatures
as happy as rats.

OUT OF THIS WORLD

I love king-sized beds in expensive hotels,
but don't give me the suite,
I want just the bed to fill the whole room,
leaving enough space for the minibar

brimming with candy and beverages,
the glimmering packages and bottles and cans,
and those slick, shiny bags of nuts
I tear open with my teeth.

I love the television meditating
in its cherry wood cabinet,
the remote ready for my commands.
I love to lie down

in the middle of the bed,
lounging against the feather pillows
towering around me like guardian angels.
I don't love the phone, so I take it off its hook

and drape my underwear over the clock radio
on the nightstand. I love books,
but there are no books here, except the Bible
hidden away like an invisibly available God.

I love the magazines fanned out,
containing no redeemable content,
only pages of nail polish
like hundreds of different ice creams:

Mauve-a-rita, Belize It Or Not,
Queen of d'Nile, Out of This World.
And when I get lonesome, I love
how my love returns from hours of Black Jack

and gin and tonics, life must go on,
but first we'll rest, so I close the thick curtains,
loving their weight and the field of wild flowers
from floor to ceiling, covering the darkness.

THE SHADY WAY INN

Six years old, you sit on the red leather bar stool swinging your legs,
eating salty peanuts from a dish, sipping a Shirley Temple

through a red plastic straw, the room dark and cool,
gold light streaming from the doorway, windows brimmed

with that gold, and the Pabst Blue Ribbon sign glowing
above the bar, its foaming glass of beer levitating

inside a waterfall. You love the dark wood of the bar,
the floor stained with spills, the fertile, sweet, dizzying

ferment of hops, your father beside you talking, gesturing,
everyone laughing, he's so funny, so handsome,

you want to marry him, you *will* marry him
when you grow up, you haven't figured out the details yet,

details like his marriage to your mother.
You could sit in this bar forever

ordering one Shirley Temple after another,
but you are hungry, so you tell your father.

He twirls you around on your stool, then picks you up
and foxtrots with you, doing his trick step,

and everyone applauds, even the bartender,
because your father is a god, he is God. The men you'll love

in your life will be cast in his image, and you will meet them all
in bars, you'll bring the cool glasses of beer to your lips,

watch the sun go down in a mirror and the windows fill with gold,
while your father tries to kill himself over and over, promising

to never drink again, you'll sit on a barstool listening,
Unforgettable on the juke box, a woman dancing with a man.

BRALESS

In September of 1970 we took off our bras
and waved them like flags over our liberated heads,
cruising in Jan's convertible Bug
to the college we would attend.
When we let the bras go, they fluttered up
on various cup-sized wings and flew
into a cornfield.

We were eighteen, we could do whatever we wanted,
and that first Friday night staring awestruck
at Tina Turner singing on the outdoor stage,
I wanted to belt out the lyrics of my life,
a life unlike any woman's I'd known.
I was free in my gauzy blouse,
dancing in the street with a man
with long curly black hair and a paisley bandana.
He quoted Nietzsche and Rimbaud,
and he knew all about Plath.

How old are you? I asked.
Let's go to a party, he said.
It was dark under the oaks by the creek,
no other cars but his station wagon.
The party's here, he said, pressing
my hand into his lap.

I told him I was a virgin,
and he held my hair back so hard
I thought my skull would crack.
He bit my neck, whispering
that he was so big,
I couldn't handle it,
but he'd know when I was ready
just by looking at me.

Thank you, I said.

As we drove to the dormitory,
he said he'd come by tomorrow.
I have homework.
You sure are a smart girl. He winked.

I locked the door of my room,
lay down in my narrow bed,
the stack of books on the desk
outlined in the light
from the streetlamp.
I would get smarter.
And if a man ever did anything
like that again,
I would do what I wanted.
I would kill him.

DEAR JOHN

Thank you for suffering blue-balls continuously for three years during marathon kissing and dry-humping on my parents' Naugahyde couch in the family room under the framed mosaic of fruit that kept falling on us while my baby sister banged her rattle nonstop against the bars of her playpen, and for the days at the beach and nights on the mountain— going together through the doors of perception—smoking marijuana, eating peyote, crushing mushrooms to mix with Ripple and chug in the Fillmore while dancing to The Jefferson Airplane, and for not making a big deal about me throwing up on your boots when Grace Slick was singing "One pill makes you larger, and one pill makes you small," and you were truly heroic the time we dropped LSD while watching *Psycho* on television and suddenly there were no walls or floor or ceiling, only endless sandless desert and your calm voice bringing me back, and for hundreds of sunsets, reasonless laughter, and your faithful listening as I tried to figure why my mom was lying by the refrigerator and what happened to my dad, thank you for helping me live less terrified, and planting the seed of the life-altering idea: a man can be a woman's friend, and I'm sorry my uncle said that weird thing about your nose before he fell into the Christmas tree and broke the window, but you handled it with grace, cleaning up the mess, and you were patient, care-fully unbuttoning the nineteen minuscule lace-covered buttons and del-icately lifting Jesus on his cross onto my shoulder and touching my flat breast like it was the Colossus of Rhodes, and I wish I'd said yes five years after high school when you appeared at Long's Drugs where I was feather dusting bags of pet food, making my slow way through college, and you were hoping I wasn't a virgin anymore, after all I'd been mar-ried and divorced, so would I consider coming to your room at Motel 6 and paying back those blue-balls I owed you, and your gold-brown eyes stayed locked on mine after I said no, and then you shrugged and solemnly smiled as though to see me was finding something in yourself you never wanted to lose, and then I almost changed my mind, but didn't, and now I'd take you to the Ritz, but I haven't seen or heard of you in twenty years, and the seed finally blossomed and I've been loving another man who is my friend, so instead I write this poem, it is a gar-land of thanksgiving for you, dear John.

AFTER BREAKING UP WITH MY
TWENTY-SEVENTH BOYFRIEND

I was alone, on vacation, as far down
in Mexico as I could get,
standing in a crowded bar.
He told me his name was Lizard King,
and asked if I wanted to see his iguana.
"Sure," I said.
He opened his guitar case and there
was an iguana wearing a sombrero with the name Carlos
stitched in red across the brim.
Carlos looked like he had a bad hangover
but seemed ready, his tiny guitar
held professionally in his scaly arms.
"Any requests, Senorita?"
Lizard King's eyes glittered
like grains of black sand, and my skin itched.
I didn't care for music anymore,
it all sounded the same.
"Play something that's not about love."
Lizard King smiled. Many of his teeth were missing.
"Si," he hissed, and Carlos began to strum
Que Sera, Sera with his claws.

CHRISTMAS EVE, 1975

Christmas is the worst: the turkey charred in the oven, someone pushed into the tree, the screaming, the crying, going to bed hoping you'll never wake up, then church the next morning, looking at your parents' hangdog, hungover faces and singing *Joy to the World*. You can't get through it this time, so you leave before dinner. You drive down the mountain, stop at The Pagoda and order takeout because you also can't bear to sit on one of those ripped red vinyl stools, hunched over the chipped formica counter with the other holiday sad sacks. You open a carton and break the plastic fork on the mound of chow mein. It is sub-zero in your car, a white Volkswagen Bug rapidly vanishing under the blizzard. You eat straight out of the carton until you can't reach the noodles with your lips, and then sputter further on toward your studio apartment, a prison cell among a block of prison cells. Now the left windshield wiper won't work, and you rise up in your seat and lean out the window to brush the snow off. You don't know how to live. You are twenty-three, divorced, working as a waitress in a restaurant called The Mallard, located between a silo and a rice swamp, where you carry so many bowls of chowder on a tray the ends of your braids become glopped with clam sauce, where the duck hunters slam down shot after shot of J.D., devour hunks of deer and beef, and slap their fat palms across your ass. You could stop at a pay phone and call your boyfriend whom you've broken up with and gotten back together with to break up with again, but you know it's better to be alone. Your body insists on being alone: every time you make love you get a bladder infection. You can't afford therapy, so you read the great books of literature, religion, philosophy. Sooner or later, you are bound to understand something. You are at the top of the final hill about to descend into Oroville, a town famous for domestic violence. Silent night, holy night. You can't see the star of Bethlehem but still believe anything can happen, even happiness.

II

THE BATTLE

As we stand on the darkling plain of the tennis court,
the Battle of the Second Set about to commence,
I remember that someone said
the most important problem we face
is restraining our own aggression,
but as the fuzzy yellow ball bounces
towards me, I want to hit the hell out of it,

and I think of the man behind the counter in the deli
who said I should try the prosciutto sandwich
and I replied, "No thanks, I want the turkey sandwich,"
but he kept on about how good, right, and true the prosciutto was,
how I ought to, I needed to, I had to
try it at least once, until I almost screamed,
GIVE ME THE TURKEY OR I AM GOING TO KILL YOU,

but I was hungry so I courteously hissed, "Excuse me,
I'd just like a turkey sandwich with mayonnaise, please,"
and wanted to add, but restrained myself, "and even
if you feel it's God's will to put tomatoes on it, don't.
As an agnostic Buddhist existentialist who loves Jesus,
I like my sandwiches plain and on sliced sourdough,
but if you only have foccacia, fine,
I realize you've been here since the birth of civilization,
you are the leader of the deli, but I'd prefer the turkey
if it wouldn't be impinging too much
on your belief in or theory of sandwiches."

The deli man flashed his incisors, then slapped
the bread down on the counter, and now
my stomach, roiling with indigestion,
is about to explode
as I stand wielding my racquet,

human and ignorant and aggressive,
ready to undercut the fuzzy yellow ball,
spin it, dink it, lob it, and slam it
down my dear friend's throat.

MY CAR

I screamed the other day when I saw a car so big
it made me think of that horror movie
about a gargantuan spider taking over a city,
and then of my first time in Costco when I saw a mayonnaise jar as big
as an eight year old child. The car was an SUV,
but at least a block long, with tinted windows
so it looked like no one was driving, and going so fast
it could tear a hole in the universe. Have you noticed
how huge the cars are getting, the maxi-vans and maxi-trucks
with elevators and escalators, a 12plex cinema, an IMAX dome?
The lost city of Atlantis could be in there, or the city the spider ate.
Soon, people will need to be hoisted by a crane to get into their cars.
The car I have now can fit under those cars, it can be flattened
in an instant.

My next car will be the biggest car in the world.
My car will carry skis, sleds, canoes, kayaks, surfboards, sailboards,
bikes, motor bikes, boats, motor boats, it will have a Stealth missile on top.
My car will be so big I will live forever.
It will take up seven lanes of freeway and all of the airspace above it.
It will be a rolling Hearst Castle, a wheeling Taj Mahal,
a barreling-down-the-road Palace of Versailles.
Honk, honk, hurry, hurry, there's a sale on everywhere
in the maxi-mini malls. Let's drain the ocean,
we need more parking lots, and have a whale
and dolphin fish fry. Just drive on over
in your Infinite Voyager, your Ubiquitous Windstar,
and we'll eat until we puke.

ODE TO HIGH SCHOOL, 1966-1970

O those four long years of being stoned
and parting my hair down the middle

and stitching the armhole of my tie-dyed dress
onto my lap in Home Ec. And the excitement

of a real date, besides trying opium with Bob and Jeff
on the railroad tracks behind the school:

Rich Lane took me to see "2001, A Space Odyssey."
We smoked a joint laced with horse tranquilizers

on the way to San Francisco, and during the movie,
I went to the restroom, and it was so interesting—

all those faucets—but how to get out, I mean,
which door? Later, Rich parked on a hill

overlooking the lights of the oil refinery and put my hand
on his penis—it felt like cement—and I yanked

the car door open and fell out, and he said, *Come on,*
you've touched a penis before, and I started walking,

Rich cruising along, his head stuck out the window, yelling, *Get in,*
your mother will kill me, but I walked the five miles home,

and my mother asked, *Is that a twig in your hair?*
Do you want to end up like Janey Miller? She had to go to Japan.

But you won't go to Japan, Missy, you'll go to a nunnery!
Grounded for two weeks, I still managed to take amphetamines and
    mescaline

and smoke hash during lunch, and learn about rocks—
O igneous, metamorphic, sedimentary—and the periodic chart,

and how many senators and congressmen and assassinated
Kennedys and civil-rights leaders and napalmed children

can dance on the head of a pin, and the galaxy slung on string
hanging from thumbtacks on the ceiling.

I wanted to go to Saturn, sit on one of its rings,
think things through. I felt old and weary,

my mind like a ball of yarn unraveling under the desks,
until one summer day after I'd graduated.

Slumped in the car in the Foster's Freeze parking lot
with an LSD hangover, I looked out the windshield

at balloons and little plastic flags, their sharp, clear
color—red, white, and blue—was it the Fourth of July?

O I had lost track of time, and who I was,
I wanted to keep her alive. I sat up.

There was a tree, the leaves moving slightly,
just a tree and leaves and that was enough.

I HAVE A HEADACHE

the size of the solar system and go to bed without any dinner
except for a bottle of water which I knock off the bedside table
while reaching to turn off the lamp, and now the carbonation
gurgles in my stomach like the bed's a deserted island surrounded
by a swamp of crocodiles, and I am thrashing in the dark,
my hands squeezing my frontal lobes because my brain
has mutated into one of those balls with spikes all over it
and is hammering its way out of my cranium on every side,
360 degrees of crushing, piercing pain,
and I have had this headache all day and headaches all
of my life and now a Godzilla one at that time of the month
every month for the past three years, and I see a headache
specialist, but look, Dr. Liang, the herbs and acupuncture aren't
cutting it, and I want morphine except I am allergic to drugs,
even aspirin, and I don't want to die although I tell Kenneth
when he comes home from working for sixteen hours
and is worried about money and sees me writhing
that I can't stand it, and the it expands to include how old I am
and I never had a baby, and how could I have had a baby,
I am a baby, I never did grow up and how could I, my parents
were babies and I still blame them, that's how much of a baby
I am, an un-self-actualized baby, and I've been teaching Freshman
Composition for twenty years and never wrote a book yet,
and we need some new furniture, and I want a dog but the fence
is falling apart, and there's no food in the house, we can't even
take care of ourselves so it's a good thing we never had a baby
and don't have a dog and yes that's the cat under the blanket,
and I know we weren't going to let the cat sleep with us
anymore but I am too undisciplined to even discipline a cat
and so tired, how does everyone do it, this living thing,
the routine, the getting up the flossing the brushing the
mouthwash and nevertheless you have gingivitis
and are on your way to dentures, don't you want to scream
your head off, and Kenneth sits down on the bed and says,
You could write a book called My Miserable Life,

and that's funny so I want to laugh but it hurts too much
and he says, Yeah, call it Original Stories from my Miserable
Life, but my life isn't miserable enough, I whine,
in fact it's wonderful in comparison to the many truly miserable
lives, and it's not very original, Then call it Unoriginal Stories
from my Miserable, Wonderful Life, he says, laughing so hard
he doubles over like he's in terrible pain himself,
and asks, Where did all these crocodiles come from?

SMALL PLEASURES, GREAT SWEETNESS

Just before dawn, the wind begins rioting,
and my love and I discuss the towering pine,
how it might crash through the roof, into our bed,

and suddenly I take pleasure in his nose,
which is small and aquiline and a fine addition to his face,
a face I have not tired of looking at in eight years.

The wind rattles the loose mouldings of the window panes
and we muse on the odds of being crushed.
I don't believe the worst will happen,

but he grew up in Denmark and knows
relentless rain, seasons of darkness,
bars that stay open all night,

and is surprised he made it past thirty—
every year is a bonus, he says.
I love his gratitude as I love the way he falls to sleep,

immediately, his nose a saxophone of breath tilted toward the stars.
Sometimes he holds my hand while he sleeps, a sweetness
that feels like grace. Wind pummels the doors

as I rise onto him and he rises into me,
the pine lurching in a green arc
like a wave about to break.

SWEARING, SMOKING, DRINKING

Sometimes I get the urge
to chug a couple of boilermakers
while chain-smoking, then burn the house down,
drive the car backward
along the railroad tracks to the Town Lounge,
slam-dunk a fuckload of martini's,
and dance shitfaced on top of the bar
until I'm dragged out and thrown
in the fountain to sink to the bottom
like a smashed penny
among the drowned wishes.
But it's my lucky legacy
to say, "No thanks, I've had enough."
Everything in moderation
is the goddamn-it-all-to-hell truth.
Fucking shit.

THOSE NIGHTS

The drinking began before dinner,
and dinner consisted of drinking,
and then there was only drinking,
nothing in the way of drinking,
and the sounds of drinking:

the father's glass set down on the counter,
the refrigerator opening,
the mother sliding the tray of ice from the freezer,
the refrigerator closing,
the ice in the glass,
the bottle pouring,
the bottle set down on the counter,
the picking up of the glass,
the clinking of ice,
those same sounds throughout the night,
and other sounds: something dropped,
something shattered,
the father bumping along the wall,
the sound of dead weight falling,
the mother weeping,
and finally, the sounds subsiding,
the listener
curled in the center of her bed,
fearing the silence
out of which the sounds would begin again.

THE KITCHEN IN DAYLIGHT

My mother ironed there,
between the oven and sink,
hanging the shirts and blouses,
dresses and trousers
from the knobs of the cupboards,
the top of the family room door.
All day, she bent over our clothes,
looking up now and then
out the window at roses,
strawberries, tomatoes—
everything she planted and raised,
the deep green maples, the light
on their big-hearted leaves.

THE CHAIR

The living room chair was on fire,
and my mother, drunk,
on the floor.
I edged my way past her,
as if she could burn me,
out the sliding glass door
and into the yard.
There were so many stars,
a terrible fire on every one.
They looked calm and steady,
arranged in an orderly constellation.
You wouldn't know, looking at our house—
shining lawn, flowers beaming, warm lights on—
that everything wasn't perfect,
except for the small fire blazing in the window.
I uncoiled the hose and dragged it
into the house, past my mother
who said, *I think my arm's broken.*
The fire hadn't spread. The chair just looked
like it had grown an orange tuft of hair.
Above the flames, on the bookshelf, pictures of the family,
everybody smiling, teeth white and straight.
I had to go back outside to turn on the water.
I didn't want water on anything that wasn't burning.
My mother still lay on the floor, her black hair gleaming,
eyelashes brushing her cheeks. I saw her tying my shoe
as I sat on my bed among dolls and puppets, my foot on her knee,
her head bowed toward me. Her hair was midnight blue,
it was so black, and smelled like lavender.
Outside, I turned on the faucet
and looked up at the sky,
listening to the water rush through the hose,
probably ruining the carpet.
There was a shooting star,
but wishing was a waste of time.

I went back into the house to put out the fire,
to get my mother off the floor
and to see what had happened to my father.

SWING

The nights our parents fought,
I would listen, terrified,
to my sister banging her head
against the crib. I'd go into her room,
pick her up, her small body hot and sweaty
from rocking on her hands and knees,
her diaper wet. I would change her, holding her
and pacing back and forth until she slept,
afraid my mother would come weaving down the hall.
If she saw me, she'd stand in the doorway,
glass of vodka in one hand, cigarette in the other,
talking crazy and sad.
One night, I climbed out my bedroom window
and ran down the street to the elementary school.
I sat in a swing, winding and unwinding the chains,
then pumped as hard and high as I could,
the world fallen away.
But I had to go home, take care of my sister.
I walked past creaking fences, growling dogs,
the jagged limbs of the trees.
Nothing was as frightening
as the people I loved.

PARADELLE FOR KERRY,
WHO SURVIVED THE CAR ACCIDENT

You didn't die when our mother died, you lived.
You didn't die when our mother died, you lived.
She is gone, take the hook out, swim away.
She is gone, take the hook out, swim away.
Our mother died, she is away, the hook gone.
Swim out, you lived, take when you didn't die.

Your debt is paid. You can have your life.
Your debt is paid. You can have your life.
Love her, but what was hers is still hers.
Love her, but what was hers is still hers.
You have paid your love. But her debt is hers.
Still hers, what was. Life is. You can.

Climb up the shore, leave the river its loneliness.
Climb up the shore, leave the river its loneliness.
Walk in sweet clover, learn from the heron.
Walk in sweet clover, learn from the heron.
Leave the shore its river. Sweet, walk the loneliness
in clover. Learn heron from the climb up.

When our mother died, she paid her debt.
The hook is hers, is what was your loneliness.
Still, you didn't die from the love. Can have.
But swim out the river. Hers is gone. Climb the away.
Heron, leave, learn; walk, shore up your life
in its clover. Take! Sweet you. You lived.

III

SMOKE

My mother held her cigarette like a scepter
between her first two fingers,
nails painted Forever Crimson.
A magnet on her refrigerator read,
Thank you for not breathing while I smoke.
She'd wave her hand majestically,
white plumes draping her like ermine.
On the tennis court, she smoked
between sets.

At sixty, she quit,
said it was like giving up an arm or leg.
Then she died, but not from smoking—
a car wreck in the afternoon.
She disappeared like smoke.

I remember her at the beach
playing cards with me,
sitting regally on a towel
in her turquoise bathing suit.
I loved the flash of her hand—
then a smoke ring
suspended in sunlight.

THE YARD

My mother's car was there, behind the chain link fence
among rows of cars no one got out of alive,

the front half of the roof smashed down to the seats,
the back a hole torn by the machine

called the Jaws of Life, bloodstains
rusted into the metal where the window had been

on the driver's side—
her Chrysler Le Baron now indistinguishable

from the other wrecks. A Doberman
slunk around crushed fenders, blown tires,

doors hanging open or ripped away.
Glass glinted on the seats, glass scattered

like a fine and radiant dust on the ground.
No wind. No sound. The dog, quietly malevolent,

guarding the yard on Pedrick Road, a strip
of cracked concrete heading south into weeds,

with a panoramic view of the flat earth
where people fall off and do not come back.

THE USE OF POETRY

Because her face is swollen, the left side bruised a dark blue.

Because a turban of gauze is wound around her head.

Because her left eye is closed, the right eye halfway open but blind.

Because her hands are bandaged, only her fingernails showing, the
    bright red polish unchipped.

Because *Her legs move sometimes* my younger sister says, not taking her
    eyes from our mother's motionless form beneath the blanket.

Because silver balloons float near the ceiling that say *We Love You* and
    Get Well Soon.

Because the balloons float a few more days until we sign the paper
    stopping the life-support.

Because a policeman brings us her purse found in the bushes along
    the freeway.

Because my sisters and I stare at the purse as if our mother is attached
    to it.

Because we take everything out, passing around her wallet, her driver's
    license, the photographs of ourselves, and then we clean her
    glasses, read her grocery list, untangle her Saint Christopher
    medal from its chain.

Because we go through her closet, putting her clothes and shoes into
    grocery bags to give to the Salvation Army.

Because we each choose a blouse, or a sweater, or one of her hats.

Because each of us has to keep something.

THE BRAIN AND THE HEART

She is brain dead, my mother. So I say to the nurse,
But her heart still beats, her chest rises and falls …

The nurse explains, *Your mother's heart will gradually stop.*
I ask, *How long is gradually?*

The nurse answers, *Six hours until she is legally dead.*
But what is legally?

I watch my mother's breath slow and cease.
I lay my head on her chest and cannot hear her heart.

I remember energy cannot be created or destroyed.
So where is my mother's breath?

I look at the ceiling.
There is something, circling.

And this mischievous feeling, this prankish joy.
So I almost get the joke.

The brain and the heart are the least of it.
I would laugh but don't want to frighten my father and sisters.

And I cry because she will not come back, not as she was.
Then there is only stucco on the ceiling.

Her body on the bed is rolled away.
In a few days, we have the funeral

and a party with family and friends.
I walk outside, drink a beer, watch

the sun set behind the roof,
her roses becoming a deeper red.

BIRTHDAY

I remember it well,
the day you were born,
my father says on the answering machine,
his voice almost sober.
It's April. I haven't seen him for a year
although he lives a town away.
I could drive there, park in front of his house,
wait for him to walk outside, past the flowering dogwood,
his white hair thinned to a few strips
standing up in the wind, his body thrust forward
like a tugboat towing his life's weighty cargo.
I could walk beside him, wanting nothing
in particular to happen, so much has happened already.
We could just keep going, the sunlight
falling on our brief lives no matter what we do.

FATHER'S DAY

No one answers, but I hear the TV's drone.
I push open the door and there's my old dad
hanging like an exhausted gymnast over the arm of the couch,
his fingers touching the floor, his pajamas on inside out.
How does he survive
the booze, the pills, the lack of food
and love? Who could love him? I love him,
but what is this? Again,
I have found him in time to take him to the hospital.
"I want to die," he cries as I fold him into the car,
and it becomes his mantra while I drive
past the bowling alley, the gun shop.
Should I stop and buy a pistol?
"I have nothing to live for," he says.
What can I say?
There is nothing to live for;
we make it up as we go along.
The earth didn't have to exist,
but here it is, and here we are,
parked in the Emergency lot.
He stares fiercely out the windshield.
I touch his hand; it's cold and scaly.
"There's always bowling," I joke.
"I don't bowl," he says.
We smile at each other.
"There's this," I say to my father.

DRIVING PAST YOUR GRAVE

I meant to stop, but you remember
how the traffic is on Fridays.
I didn't get into the slow lane in time
and missed the exit.

When I saw the East Lawn sign,
I waved like always, thinking how silly,
waving at a cemetery.
You aren't there,

but I wanted to sit under the maple.
It's Indian summer, your favorite season.
I can see you in the backyard
moving among the eighteen pine trees you planted

in our quarter acre.
Now I find only the voracious sun,
open field with crow searching
for something that shines,

the long blue sky. What's beyond,
I would not ask. I would only
sit under the changing maple
near the dates—

1928, 1989—
and the roses etched
on the headstone
above your name.

LOVE MATCH

I'm still alive, my father says, walking slowly toward me
across the tennis court,
wearing his white shirt and shorts.
His legs like thin reeds seem barely able to hold him up,
the little bit of hair left on his head fluffy
as the feathers of a baby bird. I can beat him now,
place each shot where he'll never get it.
Can't run like I used to, he says.

I hit the next ball not quite to him but close enough
so he can reach it and stroke it with his usual finesse,
low over the net, landing in the backhand corner,
causing me to nearly miss, but I don't
and return it as hard as I can
down the forehand line, to his backhand,
he's a lefty. He taught me well,
every bone in my body competitive,
forgetting that my opponent is my father
and 77 years old.

He lunges for the ball, almost falls on his face.
What's the score? he asks, limping to the service line.
Amazing, his will to keep going,
past the years of alcoholism,
the turning away of his daughters,
past the deaths of two wives,
his friends disappearing
into Alzheimer's or chronic sickness
or death, *I'm glad I woke up today,* he says,
death always present, moving closer
to me, too, evening the score.

My father makes a perfect drop shot,
and the point is his. He raises his white, bushy eyebrows,
flashes that crazy grin. He used to never lose a game,

never made it easier, taught me to fight,
and told me you're really playing against yourself.
As I stand ready to serve, my father says,
Give it all you've got, don't let up on me now.

WHEN MY MOTHER MEETS GOD

When my mother meets God,
she says, *Where the hell have you been?*
Jesus Christ, don't you care about anyone
but yourself? It's time you wake-up,
smell the coffee, shit or get off the pot.
You must have won your license in a fucking raffle.
You're grounded, and I don't want any back-talk.
In fact, don't talk at all until you can say something
that is not a lie, until you can tell the truth.
You know, the truth? Something in sentence form
that comes out of your mouth and is not a lie.
Could you do that for me? Is this possible
in my lifetime? Don't ever lie to me again
or I'll kill you. And get off your high-horse,
WHO DO YOU THINK YOU ARE? Running around the world
like a goddamn maniac, creating havoc. You have lost
the good sense you were born with. Shape up or ship out.
I can't believe we're related.

My mother lights a cigarette, pitches the match
through the strings of a harp, inhales profoundly,
letting the smoke billow from her nose.
Her ruby lips press together in a righteous grimace
of disgust. She never stops watching God.

I've really had enough this time.
What do you take me for? A fool? An idiot? A patsy?
Some kind of nothing set down on earth for your convenience,
entertainment? A human punching bag? For your information,
I was not born yesterday. I know what you're up to.
I have been around the block a few thousand spins of the wheel.
I have more compassion in my little finger
than you have in your entire body. I am a mother.
I care. Maybe you don't care, but I do. Care.
Do you know what that word means? Bring me the dictionary,

and I will tell you what the word care *means. Never mind.*
How could you find a dictionary in that dump you call a room.
The whole universe of care down the toilet
because of your dirty socks. Do I look like a maid?
Did you think the purpose of my existence was to serve you?
You are barking up the wrong tree. We need to get something
straight: I am not here for you. I am here for me.
But I care. Can you possibly, in your wildest imagination,
hold two ideas in your tiny mind at the same time?
This is called paradox. Par-a-dox. We need the dictionary.
No, we need to talk. What do you have to say for yourself?

"I'm sorry," God replies.

You're sorry. Well, that's not enough.
Wash that sullen look off your face,
or I'll wash it off for you.
And quit looking down. Look at me!

God lifts his heavy head,
falls into the fierce love
of my mother's green-blue eyes.

Grow up, she says.

IV

BUDDHA'S DOGS

I'm at a day-long meditation retreat, eight hours of watching my mind
    with my mind,
and I already fell asleep twice and nearly fell out of my chair, and it's not
    even noon yet.

In the morning session, I learned to count my thoughts, ten in one minute,
    and the longest
was to leave and go to San Anselmo and shop, then find an outdoor cafe
    and order a glass

of Sancerre, smoked trout with roasted potatoes and baby carrots and a
    bowl of gazpacho.
But I stayed and learned to name my thoughts; so far they are:
    wanting, wanting, wanting,

wanting, wanting, wanting, wanting, wanting, judgment, sadness. *Don't
    identify with your
thoughts,* the teacher says, *you are not your personality, not your ego-
    identification,*

then he bangs the gong for lunch. Whoever, whatever I am is given
    instruction
in the walking meditation and the eating meditation and walks outside with
    the other

meditators, and we wobble across the lawn like *The Night of the Living
    Dead.*
I meditate slowly, falling over a few times because I kept my foot in the air
    too long,

towards a bench, sit slowly down, and slowly eat my sandwich, noticing
    the bread,
(sourdough), noticing the taste, (tuna, sourdough), noticing the smell,
    (sourdough, tuna),

57

thanking the sourdough, the tuna, the ocean, the boat, the fisherman, the
   field, the grain,
the farmer, the Saran Wrap that kept this food fresh for this body made of
   food and desire

and the hope of getting through the rest of this day without dying of
   boredom.
Sun then cloud then sun. I notice a maple leaf on my sandwich. It seems
   awfully large.

Slowly brushing it away, I feel so sad I can hardly stand it, so I name my
   thoughts; they are:
sadness about my mother, judgment about my father, wanting the child I
   never had.

I notice I've been chasing the same thoughts like dogs around the same park
   most of my life,
notice the leaf tumbling gold to the grass. The gong sounds, and back in
   the hall,

I decide to try lying down meditation, and let myself sleep. The Buddha in
   my dream is me,
surrounded by dogs wagging their tails, licking my hands.
   I wake up

for the forgiveness meditation, the teacher saying, *never put anyone out of*
   your heart,
and the heart opens and knows it won't last and will have to open again and
   again,

chasing those dogs around and around in the sun then cloud then sun.

IN THE ART GALLERY

The painting of flowers
next to the painting of flames,
and I remember that time, years ago,
when the psychiatrist said, "You feel too much,
you are too sensitive, take these,"
giving me a bottle of pills. I took them
to the beach, watched light become flame
on the water, and along the ragged cliffs,
small flowers like blue stars,
the world a painting
I couldn't live in.
I opened the bottle, then put it down,
pills spilling on the sand.
Waves carried the flames
and didn't mind the burning,
the arising from and disappearing
into the vastness. I swam,
let the waves take me,
then treaded water, looking at the sky,
a silver tray full
of the most beautiful nothing.
I swam back, the water was black,
I could sink beyond caring,
but I wanted to live,
to be there
with the beauty and the burning
and let it be too much.

CHANCE MEETING

I know him, that man
walking toward me up the crowded street
of the city, I have lived with him
seven years now, I know his fast stride,
his windy wheatfield hair, his hands thrust
deep in his jacket pockets, hands
that have known my body, touched
its softest part, caused its quick shudders
and slow releasings, I have seen his face
above my face, his mouth smiling, moaning
his eyes closed and opened, I have studied
his eyes, the brown turning gold at the centers,
I have silently watched him lying beside me
in the early morning, I know his loneliness,
like mine, human and sad,
but different, too, his private pain
and pleasure I can never enter even as he comes
closer, past trees and cars, trash and flowers,
steam rising from the manhole covers,
gutters running with rain, he lifts his head,
he sees me, we are strangers again,
and a rending music of desire and loss—
I don't know him—courses through me,
and we kiss and say, *It's good to see you,*
as if we haven't seen each other in years
when it was just a few hours ago,
and we are shy, then, not knowing
what to say next.

FULL MOON, CABO SAN LUCAS

I've drunk enough tequila to walk into the ocean
wearing my dress and sandals,
a white flower in my hair,
singing words of a John Prine song
I don't know. My friend follows me, swirls
near the bubble of my skirt. I'm in
his arms now, floating, looking up at the stars.
We might be fish or anemones,
happy at last in our true habitat.
Then he floats in my arms,
his feet in heavy tennis shoes
splayed in a V from his ankles.
I could love this man. I could love anyone
when we are not on land, when we have no names
and hold each other like this,
almost without touching, buoyant
in the radiant, watery dark.

EASTER SUNDAY

The lawn chair is plaid and coming apart,
strips of the weave unweaving
as I bask in the last of the sunlight
I found by the door to the laundry room,
beside the anonymous bush
with the flowers petaled
like spokes of a wheel
and the crayon yellow
I knew as a child.
And now I remember
my Easter dress
and the yardage department
in J.C. Penney's basement
where my mother and I
are moving slowly down the aisles of cotton.
The sky is the color of her eyes,
and at my feet is the pile of pine needles
I swept up and forgot,
wanting the last of the sunlight
and the various songs of the birds,
especially the long clicking
that repeats every two seconds
and must be a mating call.
I'm feeling sexy
staring at the water meter,
its glinting pipes and bolts and knobs,
and at the shivering (a little wind now)
apple and silky plum.
The patch of sunlight is shrinking,
but the iris has plummeted up
among weeds and wild raspberries,
purple flames licking out of green stalks,
and it's cold now, the sun gone behind the pines,

their green darkened by dusk, time
to go inside on this Sunday
when everything is resurrecting
from winter, from memory, from loss.

HAPPY HOUR

Hungry, impatient, tired,
I wait in the rain on the filthy corner
in front of the fancy restaurant: hundreds
of cars, thousands of strangers.
But not my friend. Then I notice the young man
at the table under the awning,
stroking his head with both hands,
holding it like a crystal ball,
his head bald, or shaved close, or maybe radiated.
And then I see the stitches, the patch
of skin whiter than the rest, like a flap,
a trap door where they've opened him up, done something.
He keeps rubbing his head, smoothing every part
of his scalp, a little bit of beer left
in the bottom of his glass.
Suddenly, he looks up. His eyes burn
through my chest, eyes circled
by shadows smudging down to his cheeks.
My friend taps me on the shoulder.
Her face, so close to mine,
is immense and tilted like the world
slowly spinning off its axis. The rain,
the cars, the people, all of it
horrifying, amazing, dear.

TO MY NIGHT PALS

Tonight,
I'm dressed in my new flannel pajamas

the color of snow, featuring bears,
moose, and deer among the pines.

It's the second-to-last night of November.
I'm in bed listening to rain

on the roof and the slow, soulful piano
on KKSF's Jazz Café.

I don't want the song to end,
and I like the wind, too,

the way it rustles that strange tree
I don't know the name of outside my window.

This morning I looked
through its oddly-shaped leaves and thought,

I wasn't once, but I am alive,
and then I won't be.

Now the saxophone takes the melody
from the piano,

while wind and rain gust
against the glass.

On my pajamas
the bears sleep,

the deer sneeze,
the moose stand like Zen masters,

each with a snowflake perched
on the top of his left antler.

STAR FOOD SONATA

In the Star Food parking lot,
I listen to the last shimmers of a violin adagio
and watch a man and a woman
putting groceries away.
He bends to the shopping cart,
plucking paper bags up and over to her,
and she places each carefully in the trunk.
They work ardently,
and maybe it's the Beethoven,
but I see they are music:
they move together like one instrument,
hands perfectly tuned
to take and let go,
their bodies a symphony,
arms bowing across the twilight
where leaves flamenco
round and down.
When the groceries are stowed,
they chase each other, laughing,
throwing the keys back and forth
over the roof of the battered Rambler.
Then she opens the door inside
for him. They kiss
and drive away.

Adagio, adagio, adagio.
Let it go slow:
let me live each moment
through to its end,
let me see I will never see this again,
or this, or this,
let me hear it as music—

the soundless cadence,
shimmering rhythm between everything,
the ephemeral singing
one song, infinite movement.

FOR ROAD Z

When the sadness comes, drive north
into Colusa County, past Butte City,
a one-saloon town, and turn left onto Road Z,
and anytime is fine, but try November
when rice fields brim with first rain,
and heron and crane glide low and rest
like origami on the gold shore of reeds,
and if you're lucky, it's close to sunset,
the road turning silver, curving between
the green Coastal Range and blue Sierras,
the sky wild with changes—
pinks and purples, copper and bronze,
to dark as indigo, and then the stars.
You are moving with them, out into the open,
part of the astral traffic.

AT MOUNTAIN VIEW CEMETERY

Under the old oaks, I walk with my friend
to his father's grave.
His father drowned in the swimming pool
on a night of celebration: reconciling
with my friend's mother.
It's a long story, the way he tells it,
and after twenty years of friendship,
I've heard it before,
all our stories told at least twice.

We've been looking down quite a while,
staring at his father's name, the dates.
He was forty when he died.
I notice the sunlight on the dirt.
Sometimes I think: *that's it,*
that's what I believe in.

We climb toward the summit,
rest by the grave with the blue pinwheel,
the silver balloon that reads, *Happy Birthday.*
Sometimes I imagine the sky opening up,
and there's my mother—lounging on a cloud, smoking
a cigarette, no bandage around her head,
her hair just the way she liked it.
It's all good, she says.

My friend and I stand at the top of the mountain,
looking out on the miles of dead,
the ocean. What seems like the world's end
goes around, revolving in thin air,
attached to nothing. Sometimes I believe
in what I can only describe as *something.*
It isn't good or bad. More like the wind

raising the hair on my arms, but I'm not afraid.
More like my friend telling another story
and me listening as if it's the first time
I've heard it.

Susan Browne was born in Long Beach, California. She was educated at California State University, Chico, and the University of Colorado, Boulder. Her poems have appeared in numerous journals, including *Ploughshares, River City, The Mississippi Review* and *Gargoyle*. She was selected as the winner of the Four Way Books Intro Prize in Poetry by Edward Hirsch. She has also received awards from the Chester H. Jones Foundation, the National Writers Union, and the Los Angeles Poetry Festival. She teaches literature and writing at Diablo Valley College in Pleasant Hill, California.